PEOPLE & PLACES

Southern Africa

W9-BIN-337

Written by

Peter Brooke-Ball and Sue Seddon

Consultant Roger Murray

Illustrated by

Mei Lim and Ann Savage

SILVER BURDETT PRESS
ENGLEWOOD CLIFFS, NEW JERSEY

Series Editor Sue Seddon
U.S. Project Editor Nancy Furstinger
Designer Robert Mathias, Publishing Workshop
Photo-researcher Hugh Olliff

A TEMPLAR BOOK

Devised and produced by Templar Publishing Ltd
107 High Street, Dorking, Surrey RH4 1QA

Adapted and first published in the United States in 1989
by Silver Burdett Press, Englewood Cliffs, N.J.

Color separations by Positive Colour Ltd, Maldon, Essex
Printed by L.E.G.O., Vicenza, Italy

Library of Congress Cataloging-in-Publication Data

Brook-Ball, Peter.
    Southern Africa / written by Peter Brooke-Ball, Sue Seddon;
    illustrated by Ann Savage.
        p. cm. — (People & places)
    "A Templar book" — T.p. verso.
    Includes index.
    Summary: Text and illustrations introduce the geography, history,
people, and culture of the southern region of Africa, which is comprised
of seven different countries.
    1. Africa, Southern—Juvenile literature. [1. Africa, Southern.]
    I. Seddon, Sue.   II. Savage, Ann, ill.   III. Title.
    IV. Series: People & places (Englewood Cliffs, N.J.)
    DT729.5.B76   1988
    968–dc19   88-7587
    ISBN 0-382-09797-1   CIP
                                                            AC

Contents

WHERE IN THE WORLD?

Southern Africa is not a single country, it is a region containing seven different countries: Botswana, Lesotho, Mozambique, Namibia, South Africa, Swaziland, and Zimbabwe. The tiny kingdom of Swaziland, is the smallest, and the largest and most powerful is the Republic of South Africa. Many different groups of people live in the region. They have various cultural, social, and religious traditions, some of which go back thousands of years.

Southern Africa is a region of great contrasts. It is studded with gold and diamond mines while some of the most poorly-paid and under-privileged people in the world live there. It has vast plains of grassland, rich in wildlife, and huge desert regions where little grows. There are modern cities with skyscrapers and country villages of traditional huts.

Many of the countries of Southern Africa were European colonies until quite recently. Most have gained their independence in the last 30 years, but in South Africa the black population has not achieved equal political rights with the white population. Namibia is controlled by South Africa and is the continent's last colony.

The veld
The high, fertile plateau of Southern Africa was called the veld by the original European settlers. Veld means "field" in Dutch. It is a vast, grassy plain dotted with farms and sheep stations and has a wide variety of wildlife.

Symbols of Southern Africa

The cheetah hunts antelope on the grassy plains of the veld.
The Zulu warriors carried buffalo hide shields into battle. They are well known for their geometric designs.

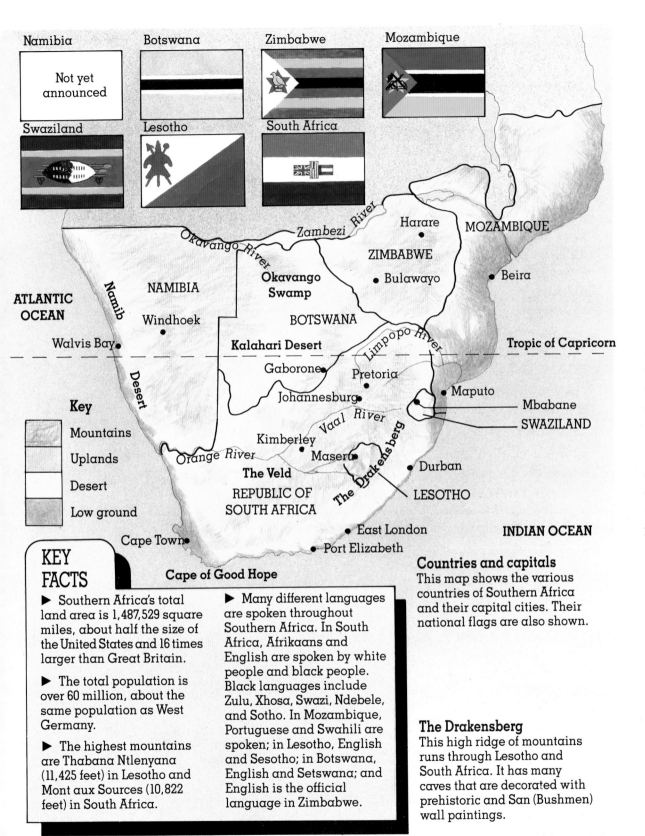

Namibia
Not yet announced

Botswana

Zimbabwe

Mozambique

Swaziland

Lesotho

South Africa

ATLANTIC OCEAN

Zambezi River

Okavango River

Harare

MOZAMBIQUE

ZIMBABWE

Bulawayo

Beira

NAMIBIA

Okavango Swamp

Namib

Windhoek

BOTSWANA

Limpopo River

Tropic of Capricorn

Walvis Bay

Desert

Kalahari Desert

Gaborone

Pretoria

Maputo

Mbabane

SWAZILAND

Johannesburg

Key

Vaal River

Mountains

Uplands

Desert

Low ground

Kimberley

Maseru

The Drakensberg

Durban

LESOTHO

Orange River

The Veld

REPUBLIC OF SOUTH AFRICA

East London

INDIAN OCEAN

Cape Town

Port Elizabeth

Cape of Good Hope

KEY FACTS

▶ Southern Africa's total land area is 1,487,529 square miles, about half the size of the United States and 16 times larger than Great Britain.

▶ The total population is over 60 million, about the same population as West Germany.

▶ The highest mountains are Thabana Ntlenyana (11,425 feet) in Lesotho and Mont aux Sources (10,822 feet) in South Africa.

▶ Many different languages are spoken throughout Southern Africa. In South Africa, Afrikaans and English are spoken by white people and black people. Black languages include Zulu, Xhosa, Swazi, Ndebele, and Sotho. In Mozambique, Portuguese and Swahili are spoken; in Lesotho, English and Sesotho; in Botswana, English and Setswana; and English is the official language in Zimbabwe.

Countries and capitals
This map shows the various countries of Southern Africa and their capital cities. Their national flags are also shown.

The Drakensberg
This high ridge of mountains runs through Lesotho and South Africa. It has many caves that are decorated with prehistoric and San (Bushmen) wall paintings.

7

A MIXTURE OF PEOPLES

The vast majority of people who live in the countries of Southern Africa today are black. Most of them are descended from Bantu-speaking tribal communities who settled in the area in the 14th and 15th centuries. Many of them have kept their own languages and traditions, such as the Zulu of South Africa, the Shona of Zimbabwe, the Tswana of Botswana and the Herero of Namibia. The original inhabitants of the region, the San (Bushmen) and the Khoikhoi (Hottentots), were gradually pushed out of the area by the Bantu-speaking tribes.

The white people, who originally came from Europe, formed separate communities and mostly married among themselves. Today, most people of European descent live in South Africa where they make up 17 percent of the population.

The South African government has introduced a system of classifying its people by racial origin: Europeans are known as "white;" the black population is categorized by tribal origin; and the people who are descended from marriages between white and black people are known as "colored." This classification is unacceptable to many people, who regard it as racial discrimination. Africans and other non-whites in South Africa prefer to be known as "black."

Asian people
The one million Asians in South Africa are descended from people brought from India by the British in the 19th century to work on sugar plantations. Most live in Natal and are Hindus.

The first settlers
Some of the first people to live in Southern Africa were the San, or Bushmen. Today, only about 50,000 San survive. They live as nomads in the Namib Desert in Namibia and the Kalahari Desert in Botswana. They move from place to place in search of food, hunting antelope with bows and arrows and spears and gathering nuts and fruits, much as their ancestors did. Their skills as trackers are used by the South African army in Namibia.

8

Clothing

Most Southern Africans who live in towns and cities wear Western-style clothes but in rural areas, many people prefer to wear traditional dress which is cooler because it is looser fitting. For special occasions and ceremonies, Zulu women wear brilliantly colored cloaks and headdresses. The headdresses are made from tiny beads woven into patterns. Each pattern tells a story.

Working together

When the first Europeans arrived in Southern Africa, contact with local people was limited. In the 19th century conflict arose over land for farming and mining. Today, white and black people live and work together in most of the countries, while even in South Africa segregation of whites and blacks has eased in recent years.

SUN, WIND, AND RAIN

Most of the population of Southern Africa lives in the southern and eastern regions. This is because much of the western and central areas are dry desert with very little rainfall. The soil is infertile and unsuitable for farming.

On the eastern side of the region conditions are very different. The high plains of the South African veld provide a cooler climate and most of the area receives plenty of rainfall for farming and crops. The rain is carried in from the Indian Ocean on warm winds and most of it falls during the wet season in the summer. To control water for irrigation, dams have been built on the mighty Zambezi River. Water from these dams is used to water crops. The dams also have hydroelectric power stations to provide cheap electricity in Zimbabwe and Zambia.

In Botswana, the Okavango River flows into the Kalahari Desert, forming a huge, marshy area called the Okavango Swamp. The land would be ideal for farming but it is a breeding area for the disease-spreading tsetse fly, which attacks cattle and humans, so consequently there are no farms.

The smoke that thunders
The Zambezi River flows over the Victoria Falls on the border between Zimbabwe and Zambia. At the falls, the Zambezi is 5,580 feet wide and drops 355 feet. The Victoria Falls were named after Queen Victoria in 1855 by David Livingstone, the explorer and missionary who was the first European to see the spectacular falls. However, the African people call them "Mosi-ao-tunya" which means "the smoke that thunders."

Pleasant climate
Cape Town, nestled under the massive Table Top Mountain, has a pleasant climate, not too hot and not too cold, which is why the first European settlers liked it so much. This is where two oceans meet. To the west, cold Atlantic currents rarely rise above a chilly 57°F, but to the east, the Indian Ocean is a warm 68°F.

▶ Southern Africa lies below the equator in the Southern Hemisphere. Its seasons are opposite to those of countries in the Northern Hemisphere. July is in the middle of winter and December is in the summer.

▶ The coast of Namibia is often covered with fog in the morning although it receives very little rain. This is because moisture is trapped in the very still air.

▶ On the high plains of Zimbabwe, the sun shines every day but the temperature is a comparatively cool 68°F.

▶ During the wet season between April and September, Mozambique is hot and humid with an average temperature of 82°F. It can be almost hard to breathe. As much as 40 inches of rain can fall during the wet season.

▶ The longest river in Southern Africa is the Zambezi which is 1,700 miles long. Close behind are the Orange River (1,300 miles) and the Limpopo (1,100 miles).

▶ Daytime temperatures in the Kalahari Desert can rise well above 86°F but at night they can drop to minus 23°F.

The Kalahari Desert
This dry region of sand dunes and rough scrubland covers an area of over 100,000 square miles – a little smaller than the state of Arizona. It covers most of western Botswana and stretches into South Africa and Namibia.

WILDLIFE WONDERS

Few regions of the world can match the variety of wildlife that is found in Southern Africa. On the plains of the veld, lions and cheetahs hunt the many species of antelope, which include the springbok and the wildebeeste. Giraffes and rhinoceroses also live on the vast grassy plains, and herds of African elephants wander from waterhole to waterhole. In the mountainous regions, there are leopards and monkeys. Southern Africa also has thousands of species of birds including vultures, flamingos, and pelicans.

Today, most of the wild animals are found in game reserves which have been created to protect them and their habitats. These reserves are run by wardens employed to keep out poachers who hunt the animals for skins. However, in times of drought many Africans living in the country are forced to kill wild animals to obtain food.

Southern Africa has an extremely rich variety of plantlife. The number of flower species alone far outnumbers those found in all of Europe.

Living stone
When it is not flowering, the Lithops cactus looks just like a pebble or small stone. The plant has two fleshy leaves which imitate the color of the surrounding soil. It grows in desert areas throughout Southern Africa.

The big cats
Lions and cheetahs hunt in different ways. Over short distances cheetahs are the fastest animals on earth. They can sprint at over 70 miles per hour while chasing their prey.

Lions, on the other hand, are slower and tend to stalk their prey until the last moment before they spring. In a family of lions, a pride, the female does most of the hunting.

Shooting with cameras

Many of the wild animals found in the region are protected species because they are comparatively rare. Tourists and visitors are driven through the game reserves to see animals in their natural habitats. They may only shoot with cameras. Among the animals they are likely to photograph are zebras, ostriches, antelopes, elephants, and giraffes.

Okavango Swamp

The Okavango Swamp in Botswana is comparatively untouched by people and is a perfect habitat for many types of animal and plant life. Crocodiles and hippopotamuses live in the many small lakes, pools, and branches of the Okavango River which are formed as it empties into the swamp.

13

FARMING ON THE VELD

Two types of farming are carried out in Southern Africa. One farm sells produce to make money, the other grows food to feed the people who farm the land. The large, modern farms of South Africa and Zimbabwe sell their produce. On small farms Africans grow crops and keep cattle just to feed the family or a village.

The main crops grown in Southern Africa are corn, sorghum (a cereal grain), cassava, sugar cane, tobacco, and many varieties of vegetables and fruit, including oranges and pineapples. Fruit growing is big business in South Africa and wine-making is a booming industry thanks to the juicy grapes that grow in the south of the country.

For every person living in South Africa, there is a sheep – more than 30 million. South Africa comes in second to Australia as a wool exporter. Most of the sheep stations are on the vast, high plains of the veld where there is plenty of good grass for grazing. The sheep are merinos, which produce very high quality wool. Some of the farms are so large that horses and motorbikes are needed to round up the sheep. There are also about five million karakul sheep, known as "black diamonds" in South Africa and Namibia. They are valued for their glossy black skins.

At home on the range
Cattle farming is important in the eastern part of Botswana and Zimbabwe and there are large cattle ranches in both South Africa and Namibia.

Put it in a pipe

Like its neighboring country, Mozambique, Zimbabwe has many tobacco plantations. Tobacco is grown for sale, mainly to overseas countries, and is sold in order to buy other goods. The tobacco leaves are hung in racks to dry before they are ground up to produce the familiar type of tobacco found in cigarettes. Zimbabwe is the third largest tobacco-producing country in the world.

Main crop

Corn is one of the most important food crops grown in Southern Africa. It forms the main diet for many Africans and the tough stalks can be used to make paper and board. Zimbabwe grows so much corn that it exports some of its annual crop to other countries in Africa.

DOWN BY THE SEA

For generations people have fished along the coast of Southern Africa, using either lines or nets. A cold current, the Benguela, sweeps up the western coast of the region and carries with it huge shoals of pilchards, anchovies, and mackerel. These days, fleets of trawlers fish the Benguela and bring their catches home to Cape Town or Walvis Bay, although Namibia's fishing industry has been badly affected by foreign fleets fishing in the same waters. Most of the fish is canned or converted to oil or fish-meal, which makes an excellent fertilizer.

On the east coast the warm waters of the Indian Ocean yield sardines and more dangerous fish such as barracuda and sharks that are hunted for sport.

Durban in South Africa has some of the most beautiful beaches in the world with long stretches of sand washed by warm water. Tourism is a big industry and many thousands of South Africans flock to the seashore every summer. However, because of the South African government's policy of racial segregation, black and white people must use separate beaches.

Fishing big

A million tons of fish are caught off Namibia and the west coast of South Africa every year by fleets of trawlers. The amount of fish landed annually is restricted by law to conserve the supply.

Rock-lobsters provide a small but profitable trade for some fishermen. They are either frozen or exported live to the United States, Japan, and France.

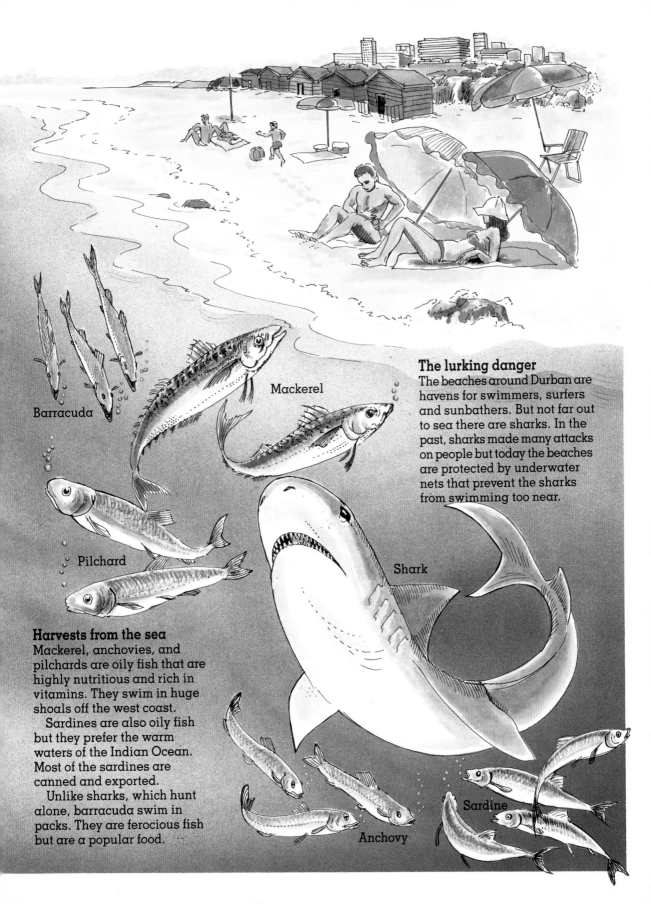

Barracuda

Mackerel

The lurking danger

The beaches around Durban are havens for swimmers, surfers and sunbathers. But not far out to sea there are sharks. In the past, sharks made many attacks on people but today the beaches are protected by underwater nets that prevent the sharks from swimming too near.

Pilchard

Shark

Harvests from the sea

Mackerel, anchovies, and pilchards are oily fish that are highly nutritious and rich in vitamins. They swim in huge shoals off the west coast.

Sardines are also oily fish but they prefer the warm waters of the Indian Ocean. Most of the sardines are canned and exported.

Unlike sharks, which hunt alone, barracuda swim in packs. They are ferocious fish but are a popular food.

Sardine

Anchovy

MINING FOR GOLD AND DIAMONDS

The first European explorers to travel inland from the west coast of Southern Africa could hardly believe their eyes when they came to a place called Pomona. In front of them the ground sparkled. They had found diamonds literally lying in the sand! Apart from some diamonds found along the shore in Namibia, valuable gems are not found lying on the surface these days but are mined from beneath the ground. Between them, South Africa, Botswana and Namibia provide the world with most of its diamonds for jewelry.

There is gold too, especially in Zimbabwe and South Africa. It has to be dug out of the ground with machinery and some of the mine shafts are almost 2 miles deep.

The black miners who work in the gold and diamond mines of South Africa and Namibia often work far from their homes. They live in special settlements near the mines. Women and children are not allowed in the settlements, so the miners have to leave their families and may only see them once or twice a year.

One mineral that Southern Africa does not have in large amounts is oil, although exploration is underway in Mozambique, Botswana, and offshore South Africa. However, it does have plenty of coal and South Africa has the world's largest plant for producing oil from coal.

KEY FACTS

▶ Diamonds are weighed in *carats*. One carat is equal to 200 milligrams. The largest, clearest, and best-shaped stones are worth the most money.
▶ The purity of gold is measured in karats. 24 karat gold is 100 percent pure, 12 carat gold is half gold and half another metal such as silver or copper.
▶ Zimbabwe has a great variety of minerals and mines 70 different kinds including gold, asbestos, copper, and tin.
▶ The largest diamond ever found was the Cullinan diamond which came from South Africa. It weighed over 3,000 carats before it was cut to make several gems. The Star of Africa – a diamond about the size of a golf ball – was just one gem cut from the Cullinan and is now in the British royal sceptre.
▶ For every ounce of gold, about three or four tons of rock have to be dug out of the earth, usually by hand with a pneumatic drill.

Before and after

When diamonds come out of the ground, they look like transparent stones. It is only when they are "cut" that they begin to sparkle. The only things that can cut or chip diamonds are other diamonds because they are so hard. There is a great art to cutting a diamond –

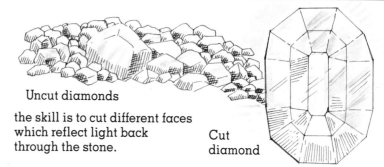

Uncut diamonds

the skill is to cut different faces which reflect light back through the stone.

Cut diamond

18

The Big Hole

The largest man-made hole in the world lies at Kimberley in South Africa. In 1869, it was a hill but as news spread that diamonds had been found there, fortune hunters dug up the ground and created the vast hole which is 2,480 feet deep. Today, the hole is flooded and it is exhausted of diamonds.

Dangerous work

Conditions down in a mine are often cramped and hot and the work is difficult and dangerous. Miners use hand-held machinery to cut through the rock containing the gold or diamonds. Here a miner works in Zimbabwe.

TRADING WITH THE WORLD

The seven countries of Southern Africa trade with each other and with countries in other parts of the world. Mozambique and South Africa handle much of the region's overseas trade because they have most of the coastline and the best ports.

The bustling docks at Maputo and Beira in Mozambique are linked by railway to Swaziland, Zimbabwe, and eastern South Africa. Imports to, and exports from, these countries pass through Mozambique. However, South Africa handles most of the international trade, and goods from all over Southern Africa pass through the busy ports of Cape Town and Durban.

South Africa also accounts for much of the trade between the seven countries. It is by far the richest and can afford to buy minerals and other raw materials from its neighbors for its industries, in return for food products and consumer items such as refrigerators and televisions. To keep its neighbors friendly, South Africa has invested money in manufacturing and tourism in countries such as Lesotho and Swaziland. The other countries of Southern Africa have grouped together with Tanzania and Zambia to increase trade and reduce economic dependence on South Africa.

Trading difficulties

Some countries outside Southern Africa have stopped trading with South Africa because they do not agree with its policy of racial segregation. Individual foreign companies also refuse to import South African goods and some large foreign companies have shut down their factories and offices in South Africa to protest the white government's policies.

The gold capital

Johannesburg is the world center for gold mining. This city is also the banking and industrial center of South Africa. It also has Southern Africa's largest and busiest international airport. Zimbabwe's capital, Harare, a busy cosmopolitan city, is its closest rival.

Going out, coming in

Durban is the busiest port in Africa and handles more than 30 million tons of imports and exports annually. It mainly deals with mineral and textile exports and imported machinery. Cape Town, which handles about 10 million tons every year, chiefly exports processed foods, fruit and vegetables.

Monster railroads

All the major cities in Southern Africa are linked by railroads that cross the international boundaries. Most import and export goods are transported to and from the seaports by train.

Exports of Southern Africa		
Country	**Products**	**Trading partners**
Botswana	diamonds, meat, meat products, nickel, copper	South Africa, Great Britain, Switzerland, Zimbabwe
Lesotho	wool, mohair	South Africa
Mozambique	cashew nuts, copra, cotton, sugar, coal	Portugal, South Africa, East Germany, West Germany, India, Zimbabwe
Namibia	diamonds, uranium, minerals, meat, pelts, fish products, sheep	South Africa, West Germany, Great Britain, United States, Japan, Switzerland, Belgium
South Africa	gold, platinum, diamonds, coal, uranium, steel, other minerals, fruit and vegetables, textiles, wool, machinery	Great Britain, United States, Japan, West Germany
Swaziland	sugar, wood pulp, asbestos, fruit, coal	South Africa, Great Britain, United States, Japan, Kenya
Zimbabwe	tobacco, gold, coal, copper, cotton, steel, meat, corn	South Africa, Great Britain, United States, West Germany, Botswana, Mozambique

BEFORE THE EUROPEANS

The earliest inhabitants of Southern Africa were the San (Bushmen). Two thousand years ago, however, people living in northwest Africa who spoke the Bantu language moved south in search of more land. They eventually arrived in Southern Africa.

The San were hunters who wandered throughout the region in search of antelope and other animals. They also searched for roots and berries to eat. The newcomers were different – they settled in one place, herding cattle and farming crops. Bit by bit, they pushed the San out of their traditional hunting grounds and forced them into the Kalahari Desert where they have remained ever since.

As the Bantu-speaking people moved south, they split up into groups or tribes, each of which developed its own culture and traditions. Today, these tribes, such as the Zulus of South Africa and the Shona of Zimbabwe, have different languages, customs, and dress, but they are distantly related and they still speak variations of the language their ancestors spoke 2,000 years ago.

The Khoikhoi

The Khoikhoi (Hottentots) (right) were a group of people similar to the San but instead of hunting animals, they grew crops and herded cattle. They were the people whom the first Portuguese explorers met when they landed at the Cape of Good Hope. Today, there are no true Khoikhoi left as they have married into other groups. Versions of their unique language, which sounds like a series of clicks to Western ears, survive in South Africa and Namibia.

Cave paintings

The San who lived in Southern Africa thousands of years ago were remarkable artists. Many examples of their paintings can be seen in the caves of the Drakensberg in South Africa, the Brandberg Mountains in Namibia, and throughout Botswana.

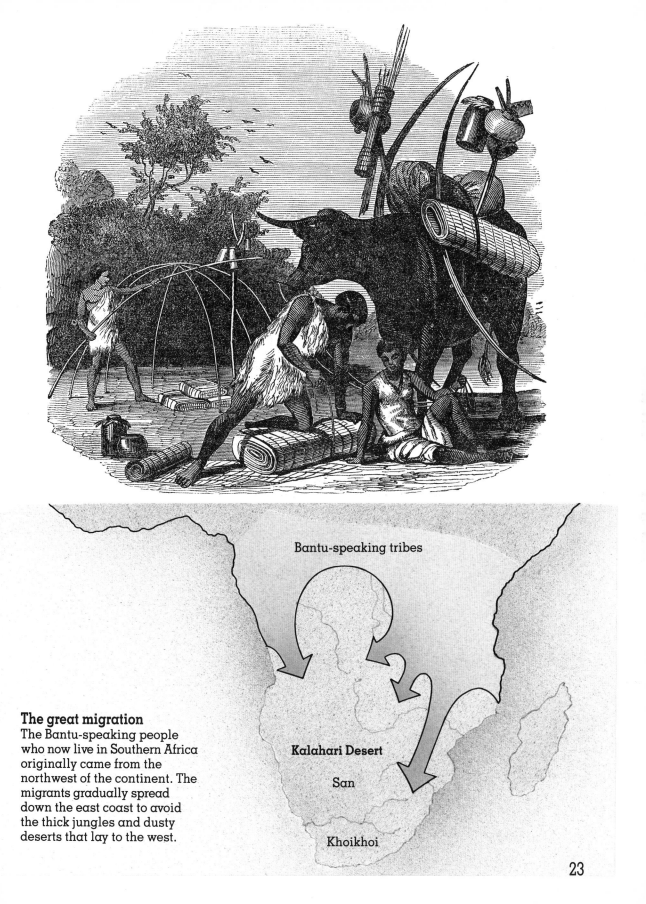

The great migration
The Bantu-speaking people who now live in Southern Africa originally came from the northwest of the continent. The migrants gradually spread down the east coast to avoid the thick jungles and dusty deserts that lay to the west.

Bantu-speaking tribes

Kalahari Desert

San

Khoikhoi

23

THE EUROPEANS ARRIVE

The first Europeans to visit Southern Africa were Portuguese explorers who sailed round the Cape and mapped the coastline at the end of the 15th century. The Portuguese began to colonize what is now Mozambique at the beginning of the 16th century. They built a series of forts along the coast in which they collected valuable cargo ready to be shipped back to Europe. They traded in ivory and gold but the most valuable cargo of all was black slaves. Some slaves were shipped to Europe, but most were sent to North and South America.

The Dutch were the first Europeans to settle the region that is now South Africa. They began a settlement around the Cape of Good Hope in 1652 to provide food and water to trading ships on their way to the Far East. Over the next 200 years they established a colony. The Dutch settlers called themselves "Boers," meaning farmers. As their population grew they spread inland and took land from the African people who, in turn, retreated further inland and fought each other for the remaining land. Thousands of Africans died in the battles for land.

In 1795, the British arrived in South Africa in search of new land to colonize. Eventually, to get away from British rule, the Boers left their settlements around the Cape and travelled inland to find new land to farm.

The Great Trek

To escape British rule 10,000 Boers left the region around the Cape in the mid-1830s. They trekked inland through unknown country in traditional covered wagons drawn by teams of 16 oxen. The search for new farmland was often dangerous as the Africans tried to stop the Boers from taking their land. The Boers finally set up two independent states, the Transvaal and the Orange Free State.

Great Portuguese explorers

Five hundred years ago, Bartolomeu Dias (also called Bartholomew Diaz) was the first European to sail around the southernmost tip of Africa. He called it the Cape of Tempests, but it was later renamed the Cape of Good Hope. Dias is known to have set foot in Southern Africa at Dias Point in Namibia. In 1498, Vasco da Gama was the first European explorer to visit the coast of what is now Mozambique during his search for a sea-route to India.

Key Vasco da Gama   – – – – –

Bartolomeu Dias   – · – · – ·

Bartolomeu Dias

Vasco da Gama

The slave trade

The Arabs who had spread down the east coast from the Red Sea area were the first slave traders. When the Portuguese arrived in the 16th century many of them became slave traders. Thousands of black men, women, and children were captured, herded onto ships and transported in appallingly overcrowded conditions to the Americas where they were sold as slaves, mostly to work on the land. The trade in slaves from Southern Africa lasted nearly 400 years.

25

THE SCRAMBLE FOR EMPIRE

Just over 100 years ago, all the powerful countries of Europe wanted to claim parts of Southern Africa. They wanted to expand their empires and to obtain the valuable deposits of gold and diamonds found there. Germany colonized Namibia, or South West Africa as it is still called by South Africa, but surrendered it to South Africa during World War 1. South Africa has occupied Namibia ever since, although since 1947 the United Nations has demanded it be given its independence.

The British claimed the areas that are now Botswana, Lesotho, Zimbabwe, and South Africa. The Boers and the British constantly disagreed over ownership of South African land and mining rights and this led to the Boer War. The British finally overcame the Boers in 1901. At first, the British ruled the country and controlled the gold and diamond mines. Eventually they allowed the Boers, now known as Afrikaaners, to govern themselves. Most black people were controlled by the whites and worked as cheap labor in the mines.

One of the most powerful men in South Africa during the 1880s and 1890s was the mining millionaire and statesman Cecil Rhodes. He developed the northern part of Southern Africa for Britain. It was named Rhodesia after him. At independence the country was renamed Zimbabwe after the ancient African civilization that once flourished here.

The relief of Mafeking
During the 1899-1901 Boer War, the small British garrison town of Mafeking was besieged for seven months by the Boers. When help eventually arrived for the British, crowds back in England cheered the news. The commander of the British forces was Robert Baden-Powell who later formed the Boy Scout movement.

Settling down

When they weren't fighting each other or the Zulus, the European settlers formed small farming communities on the veld. The Boers built their farmhouses in a distinctive Dutch style and many of them are still standing today.

A great general

At the beginning of the last century, several Zulu tribes were united into one nation by a Zulu warrior chief called Shaka. Under his ruthless command, the Zulus went to war to gain land in Southern Africa. He was eventually assassinated by his brother, Dingaan, after waging long wars against neighboring tribes.

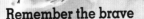

Remember the brave

After Shaka's death, the Zulus attacked the Boers and the British who were invading their lands. At Rorke's Drift, a tiny settlement on the banks of a river, 4,000 Zulus attacked some 110 British soldiers. After a day's fighting, 350 Zulus were killed and the rest fled. The British lost 17 men. The vastly outnumbered British soldiers won 11 Victoria Crosses for their bravery.

POWER AND INDEPENDENCE

On April 18, 1980, crowds gathered in all the towns and cities of Zimbabwe. They were waiting for the news that their country had gained independence from Britain. For nearly 100 years Britain had ruled several countries in Southern Africa, but by 1980 all the colonies had gained their independence. Zimbabwe was the last. The former British colonies of Lesotho, Botswana, Swaziland, and Zimbabwe remain members of the British Commonwealth – an association of independent states linked by the fact that they were once ruled by Britain.

Mozambique was not a British colony; it was once ruled by Portugal and only gained its independence in 1975, after a long guerrilla war.

South Africa was once ruled by Britain and was once a member of the Commonwealth, but left it in 1961 because of criticism of its policy of racial segregation. It is by far the most powerful country in the region and is governed by white people. Most of the other six countries are mainly dependent on South Africa for trade but they are trying to break free of its influence because they do not agree with the way in which it is governed. They want all adult black South Africans to have the vote. This would bring about a government that would represent all people in South Africa.

Sir Seretse Khama
Sir Seretse Khama (1921-1980) was the first president of Botswana. He trained as a lawyer but founded the political party that gained independence for Botswana in 1966. He was re-elected president of Botswana three times.

Great She-Elephant's choice
The present king of Swaziland, Mswati III, who was educated at a boarding school in England, came to the throne in 1986. His father had over 600 children and Mswati was chosen to be king by *Dzwelie*, (the Great She-Elephant), who was the most senior of his father's 100 wives.

The homelands

In the 1970s, South Africa created ten so-called "homelands." These are regions set aside within South Africa where black people of the same tribe are obliged to live. They are only allowed into towns and white areas to work. Black people may own land in the homelands. Four of these homelands are supposed to be self-governing but in practice they are controlled by South Africa – no other countries have recognized their independence. They are seen by many people in the world as places to confine the black population and keep them from forming a government for South Africa as a whole.

The "independent" homelands

Venda

Bophuthatswana

SOUTH AFRICA

Transkei

Ciskei

Key

"Independent" homelands

KEY FACTS

▶ Botswana used to be called Bechuanaland. It became an independent country within the Commonwealth in 1966.
▶ Lesotho is completely surrounded by South Africa. It became an independent country in 1966.
▶ Namibia is trying to gain independence but at the moment South Africa controls the way in which Namibia is governed.
▶ Swaziland is the smallest country in the region and is the only one ruled by a king. It became independent in 1968.
▶ Zimbabwe used to be called Rhodesia. It changed its name at independence. Zimbabwe is an African word meaning "stone house."

Time off

Children play a game of netball in the Transkei, one of the homelands.

TROUBLED TIMES

Although most of the population of Southern Africa is black, many of the countries have been, or are still ruled by white people. This often leads to problems, sometimes to guerrilla war.

In Mozambique the Mozambique Liberation Front (FRELIMO) fought a ten year guerrilla war for freedom from Portuguese rule. FRELIMO won their struggle for independence in 1975. In Zimbabwe, guerrillas began a bitter and bloody attack on the government in the 1960s. It ended in independence in 1980. The struggle for freedom continues in Namibia where the South West Africa People's Organization (SWAPO) is fighting for independence from South Africa.

Nearly three-quarters of the population of South Africa are black but the country is ruled by white people. The white government follows a policy called "apartheid" which means "apartness" in Afrikaans. Under this system, black people do not have the vote, nor can they live where they please. In cities they have to live in areas called townships, set aside for black people. Many people rebel against these restrictions, sometimes violently. Most countries around the world support the black South Africans in their quest for freedom but the white government has, so far, refused to change its policies.

The Sharpeville Massacre
In March 1960 a large crowd of black people gathered in the small South African town of Sharpeville. They were peacefully demonstrating against the introduction of "pass laws" which prevented blacks from going into white parts of the town. Police fired on the crowd, killing at least 60 people and wounding many more. The anniversary of the massacre is remembered by many people each year.

30

Leader of Zimbabwe

Robert Mugabe (below) was a teacher when he helped start the Zimbabwe African National Union (ZANU) in 1963. ZANU, together with another guerrilla group, waged guerrilla warfare against the Rhodesian government for nearly 20 years. Robert Mugabe was ZANU's leader. ZANU was finally recognized as a political party by the British and Mugabe was elected to be Prime Minister of the newly independent Zimbabwe in 1980.

Desmond Tutu

The Archbishop of Johannesburg, Desmond Tutu, (shown above) has spoken out against apartheid for many years. His fight against racial injustice is recognized throughout the world. He has been awarded the Nobel Peace Prize.

Anti-apartheid

Within South Africa the black and colored population is putting pressure on the government to change its policies. Many white South Africans are also against apartheid. However, most peaceful forms of protest were banned under sweeping "emergency" powers introduced in 1986. The army and police could arrest and imprison anyone thought to be guilty of violent actions without a trial in a court of law. Segregation continues; here whites and blacks sit separately in an arena.

31

UNDERSTANDING YOUR NEIGHBORS

Hundreds of different languages are spoken in Southern Africa by the various African communities. Many of these languages are related to each other and some languages are understood by several major African tribal groups. The San, like the Khoikhoi speak a distinctive "click" language made up of click sounds.

English is the most commonly understood language. It is widely spoken in all the seven countries except Mozambique, where Portuguese is the official language.

In South Africa and Namibia, Afrikaans is spoken by three out of every four white people. It is based on the Dutch language but it has been changed and added to by French, German, and British immigrants. Afrikaans did not become a written language until 1875.

Many of the people in the region are Christians. In the more remote areas, some people follow traditional beliefs. In Mozambique one in ten people is Muslim, a religion that was introduced by Arab traders about 1,000 years ago. There is also a Hindu Asian community in Mozambique whose ancestors came from the Portuguese colony of Goa in India.

KEY FACTS

Each of the seven countries has at least one official language which is used for social communication and for carrying out business.

▶ Botswana's national language is Setswana, although the official language is English.

▶ Sesotho and English are the official languages of Lesotho.

▶ The official language of Mozambique is Portuguese although it is not spoken much in the countryside. There are 12 major African communities in Mozambique and more than 30 minor ones.

▶ Afrikaans and English are the two official languages of South Africa. However, the main African languages of Zulu, Xhosa, and Sotho are most widely spoken.

▶ In Swaziland, English and siSwati are the official languages.

▶ English is also the official language of Zimbabwe, although Shona and Ndebele are also spoken.

▶ In Namibia, Afrikaans, English, and German are the official languages and more than 8 African languages are spoken as well.

Using the airwaves
All the countries in Southern Africa have national radio stations that broadcast programs in a variety of languages. The Zimbabwe Broadcasting Corporation has four radio channels catering to different languages, education, and entertainment. Botswana has a radio service but no television service of its own.

The spread of Christianity

When the European settlers first came to Southern Africa, they brought their religion, Christianity, with them. Many of the black people were converted from their traditional beliefs by missionaries, and Christian churches are now found all over the region.

Ancient beliefs

Many Africans respect nature because they believe that powerful spirits dwell in such things as rocks, trees, the wind, and the rain. They directly connect their well-being with that of their physical surroundings. However, some of their farming techniques are destroying the environment.

TRADITIONAL HOMES AND CITIES

There are many different ways of life in Southern Africa. People may live in a city or in the country. The San, who wander from place to place in search of food, do not build houses because they never stay in one place long enough. If they are hunting near caves they may live in them; if not, they rig up shelters from whatever is available, such as twigs, grass, or old sacks. Often they just sleep in the open. African rural communities live in villages of small huts, usually made from natural materials.

The modern cities of Southern Africa, such as Bulawayo, Maputo, and Cape Town, are similar to European or American cities. They have stores, restaurants, offices, churches, factories, and government buildings.

On the edges of the big industrial cities of South Africa, there are often sprawling townships for urban black people. Townships are often overcrowded with poor-quality housing and no running water.

German houses
In Namibia, where there were many German settlers before World War I, the towns of Windhoek and Swakopmund on the coast have many attractive German-style houses.

Village houses
In African villages the huts are nearly always round and are built from mud and sticks. The roofs are conical and thatched with grass. A village is usually built around a cattle *kraal* (pen) or a central meeting place that has a huge tree in the middle. On the outskirts of the village lie the fields and grazing areas.

Harare

Harare (above) is the capital city of Zimbabwe. It is a bustling, modern city with movie theaters, office buildings, and apartment houses.

Black township

Soweto is a designated black township on the outskirts of Johannesburg. Although it sounds like a Bantu word, Soweto actually means SOuth WEst TOwnship. It is the largest township, with over one million inhabitants and the center of black political opposition to the white government. It was the scene of serious riots in June 1976 when more than 100 people died.

BARTERING AT THE MARKET

Although large towns have stores and supermarkets where people can buy food and household goods, people who live in small towns and villages usually shop in markets. A Southern African market is a busy place, packed with people talking to friends and neighbors, and bargaining. Markets sell many different kinds of goods such as fruit, vegetables, domestic animals, cloth, and household goods. They are colorful too; fruit and vegetables such as oranges, pineapples, grapes, peppers, and heaps of corn are arranged in stalls or on the ground, alongside brilliant, printed cloth for traditional clothes.

At one end of the market there is usually an area where goats, chickens, sheep, and cattle are sold. Although they are sold to be eaten, shoppers usually like to buy the animals live to make sure that the meat is very fresh. They are usually killed and butchered at home. Markets near the coast have fish stalls as well.

It is customary to haggle over prices at the market – nobody accepts the price the stall holder asks without an argument. Sometimes goods are bartered or exchanged without any money being given. For example, someone may exchange a cooking pot or shawl for a goat or two hens. Items such as radios or car tires are usually sold for cash.

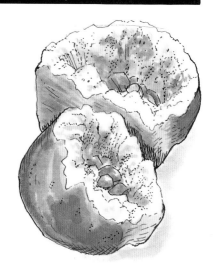

"Bunny chow"
Indian food is common in South Africa and Mozambique. A favorite meal in South Africa is "bunny chow." This consists of a half loaf of bread with the middle torn out so that the crust forms a bowl for stew or curry.

Biltong drying

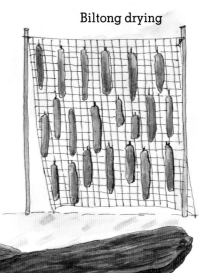

Everlasting meat
Fresh meat doesn't stay edible for very long in a hot climate but if it is cured and dried it will last indefinitely. Biltong is sun-dried meat which is cut into strips. It is very nourishing but extremely chewy.

Biltong

The meeting place

Markets are important to the people who use them because they are places where news, gossip, and information are shared. People go to meet their friends and to find out what is going on in the world as well as to buy or sell goods.

Porridge

Meat is an important part of African meals, although some African communities have a mainly vegetarian diet. A traditional meal consists of cornmeal porridge with beef stew poured over the top. In country districts the "porridge" is cooked in huge round pots over an open fire.

CULTURE AND SPORTS

The African communities of Southern Africa have a long tradition of art and culture. Artisans from all over the region still carve intricate wooden masks, statuettes, and bowls in much the same way as their ancestors did generations ago. They use only a few simple tools and often use their feet to hold the blocks of wood steady as they work. In Lesotho and Mozambique many market stalls sell mohair sweaters and rugs which are made locally. Pottery, cloth, basketware, and jewelry are made throughout the region.

One of the most famous craft centers is near the old battle site of Rorke's Drift in South Africa. Here, Zulu artisans weave colorful tapestries depicting scenes from folklore or everyday life. The Zulus are well-known for their geometric designs and these can be clearly seen on the warrior shields which are made from ox-hide.

Sports such as track and field, golf, rugby, and cricket are played in South Africa but few international competitions are held. Many other nations will not compete with a country that has a policy of separating black people from white people.

Dancing for war
Few spectacles are as awe inspiring as a Zulu battle dance. Ranks of warriors rhythmically hammer their shields with their short stabbing spears and stamp on the ground with their feet. Nowadays these dances are held for entertainment but in the old days they were designed to build up the courage of the warriors and to make enemies afraid. It is said that the great Zulu chief, Shaka, made his warriors stamp on prickly thorns to toughen the soles of their feet.

Rugby and soccer
The South African rugby team is called the Springboks after the quick and agile antelope. Sports such as rugby, cricket, and tennis were introduced by the British but soccer is the game most widely played by Africans. Here a soccer match is played in Botswana.

Music without instruments

Traditional African songs are sung by large groups or choirs throughout Southern Africa. The voices sing in harmony and are often used instead of instruments to provide rhythmical sounds. The music of the South African townships is extremely popular in Southern Africa and also in Europe and the United States. This is a group called *Ladysmith Black Mambazo*.

HEALTH AND EDUCATION

The countries of Southern Africa are working hard to improve health care but the poorer countries still do not have enough doctors, nurses, and hospitals. In Mozambique, for example, many children die of malnutrition and disease. Although South Africa has some of the best-equipped hospitals in the world much less is spent on health care for black people than is spent on white people.

Most African parents regard education as extremely important but cannot always send children to school. In South Africa and Namibia state schools are free. All white children have to go to school, but black and colored children do not. There are separate schools for blacks, colored, and whites. State-run schools for blacks are not as well equipped as those for whites, and only a small proportion of pupils complete secondary schooling. In Swaziland and Zimbabwe there aren't enough schools to educate everyone, but more schools are being built every year. In Botswana most primary school children enjoy free education.

Botswana, Lesotho, and Swaziland have set up two universities accepting students from all three countries. South Africa has 16 universities of which ten are for whites only, the rest are for different black tribal groups. Namibia has no university and students have to go to South Africa or abroad.

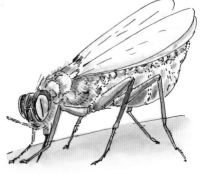

The killer fly

One of the most feared insects in Southern Africa is the tsetse fly. It feeds on the blood of animals, especially cattle and humans, and spreads disease in both. Cattle die from a disease called nagama and humans can die from sleeping sickness. Sleeping sickness can be treated with drugs but so far, all attempts to destroy the tsetse fly have failed.

New heart for old

In December 1967, Doctor Christiaan Barnard won the race to be the first person to carry out a heart transplant on a human being. The patient subsequently died but the operation made the surgeon world famous and led the way for similar operations in other countries. Many heart transplants have now been undertaken at the Groote Schuur Hospital in Cape Town.

Receiving help

International relief agencies like the Save The Children Fund help countries like Mozambique by sending out specialized workers. Some of these are doctors and nurses who face an extremely difficult task as they struggle to fight the effects of malnutrition and disease. Drugs, medicines, and food are in short supply because of lack of money.

Vaccination centers have been set up to immunize people against such killer diseases as cholera, hepatitis, and measles.

Learning to write

In Namibia and Mozambique only one in 12 people can read and write. Mozambique has launched an ambitious project designed to teach 100,000 people to read each year. It is doing this with the aid of other nations. The school below is in Namibia.

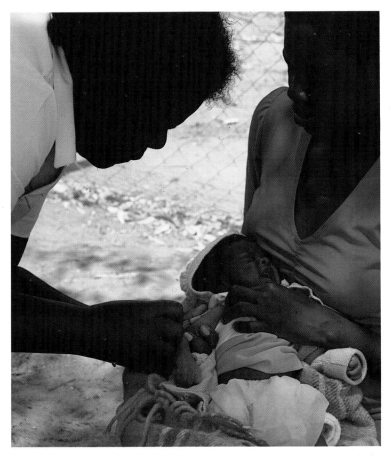

WAYS OF LIFE

T he various peoples of Southern Africa live very different lifestyles. People who live in cities lead lives much like Europeans or Americans. Many have a high standard of living, although in South Africa these people are almost all white. White people also live in the country. They are usually farmers who own large farms.

In the black townships of South Africa most adult men must work long hours in the mines or industries of the neighboring cities. Women sometimes work as domestic servants in white areas of the cities.

The majority of people who live in rural districts of Southern Africa live in small towns and villages. Many such places do not have electricity or running water, although governments are gradually improving services. People work on the land growing crops or work in local factories. They also prepare food and collect water. Children who aren't in school do household chores, look after very young children, and collect water and firewood. Community bonds are important in village life and the old and sick are looked after by their relatives or friends.

Settling disputes
Small villages often consist of only one or two families. However, some families are large and consist of children, parents, grandparents, and great-grandparents, to say nothing of aunts and uncles. If a quarrel breaks out between two people or two families, it is the task of the chief of the village to sort out the problem. His word is normally accepted by everybody.

Pounding for supper

Preparing food is often very hard work. Corn has to be pounded into flour or meal using wooden poles. Groups of women often team up to make the work easier. The corn meal is made into porridge.

Town life

Houses in the white suburbs of some South African cities are large. They often have swimming pools.

SOUTHERN AFRICA'S FUTURE

The countries of Southern Africa face severe political and economic problems. Many people fear that the tensions in South Africa could explode into a general war which would suck in all the neighboring countries. The white government has recently made a few reforms to its policy of apartheid. It still refuses to allow every adult to have the vote because the blacks outnumber the whites and would be able to choose the government. Most black political organizations are banned and many influential black leaders such as Nelson Mandela have been in prison for years. Many whites are unhappy about the situation and would like to see a multiracial government in power.

The poorer countries of the region, such as Mozambique and Lesotho, face problems of a different kind. Poverty, starvation, and disease are a continual threat. Mozambique relies heavily on aid from both Western and Communist countries but is trying to become more self-sufficient. Botswana, Swaziland, and Zimbabwe have used the income from their rich mineral deposits to build up more modern economies but many of the people living in the country are still very poor. All the countries are encouraging foreign companies to invest money to provide income for improving health and education so that the next generation will be more able to cope with the problems.

Trying to talk
The United Nations has tried to negotiate a fair independence settlement for Namibia with the support of the major world powers. The UN adopted a resolution in 1978 that would enable the country to gain its freedom by holding elections and establishing a ceasefire in the war between SWAPO guerrillas and South African troops. The South African government has yet to carry out this ruling.

Symbol of the fight for freedom
Nelson Mandela has become the symbol of black South Africa's fight for civil rights and majority rule. He trained as a lawyer, then became a national organizer of the now banned African National Congress (ANC), a political organization. In 1964 he was imprisoned for his political activities and has been in prison ever since. There has been a world-wide campaign for his release. He has been awarded many honors by organizations outside South Africa for his dignified stand for black rights.

Exploiting nature

Zimbabwe has some of the most beautiful countryside in Africa which it wants to exploit for tourism. The government of Zimbabwe is determined that the money that comes into the country should be used for the benefit of everybody – to build hospitals and schools and to encourage agriculture.

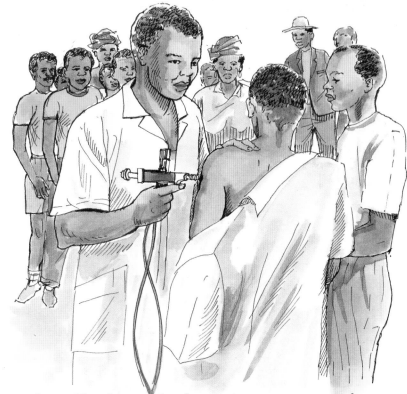

Aid and self help

Lesotho and Mozambique rely on aid from the rest of the world with which to build hospitals and schools. Money is also put aside to train doctors and teachers and to buy essential equipment such as tractors. Swaziland now makes its own cheap tractors which poor farmers can more easily afford than expensive foreign machines. The ultimate aim of these countries is to be self-sufficient and to develop their own human resources and modern technology so that they don't need help from outside.

Index

Acknowledgments

Map illustration page 7 by Ann Savage. All other illustrations by Mei Lim. Photographic credits (a = above, b = below, m = middle, l = left, r = right): Cover al W Fritz/Zefa, bl Robert Harding Picture Library, ar H D de Bruin/Zefa, br Zefa; page 8 R Ian Lloyd/Hutchison Library; page 10 Starfoto/Zefa; page 11 al H D de Bruin/Zefa; bl Robert Harding Picture Library; page 13 a Zefa, b Robert Harding Picture Library; page 15 a Robert Harding Picture Library, b Lesley McIntyre/Hutchison Library; page 16 Roger Evans/Robert Harding Picture Library; page 19 Hutchison Library; page 20 Robert Harding Picture Library; page 21 H Ballantyne/Zefa; page 22 Carol Jopp/Robert Harding Picture Library; page 23 Mansell Collection; page 27 Robert Harding Picture Library; page 28 Andrzej Sawa/Camera Press; page 29 Robert Cundy/Robert Harding Associates; page 31 a Popperfoto, b Zefa; page 33 Zefa; page 35 a Robert Harding Picture Library, b Zefa; page 37 a G M Wilkins/Robert Harding Picture Library, b W Fritz/Zefa; page 39 a Zefa, b Rex Features; page 41 a Liba Taylor/Hutchison Library, b Robert Harding Picture Library; page 43 Hutchison Library; page 45 Zefa.